Have You Seen a Friendly Robot?

By
Elaina Ashton
Anna Prakash-Ashton Ph.D.

Illustrated by
Ron Coleman

Just Empower LLC
https://just-empower.com
Email: info@just-empower.com

Ordering Information: Quantity sales. Special discounts are available on quantity purchases by corporations, associations, and others. For details, contact the publisher at the address above.

ISBN (paperback): 978-0-578-76523-5
ISBN (ebook): 978-0-578-89051-7

Acknowledgements

Our sincere thanks to:

Standout Books publishing services

Fiverr team for Spanish translations

Tommy Ashton II and Ethan Ashton
& Fiverr team for audio book conversions

A portion of all proceeds supports our nonprofit, Education Empowers Inc. (www.educationempowers.org)

Table of Contents

Robots Are Here!

Did you know that robots are machines made by humans that can sense, perceive (understand), plan, and act? Robots are problem-solvers, capable of carrying out actions automatically, and they can be programmed by a computer. They come in many shapes, sizes, and forms!

Did you know that you can find robots in every field of work, from medicine and construction to manufacturing, space exploration, and even entertainment? Robots are machines made by humans that can sense, perceive (understand), plan, and act. They are problem-solvers and come in all shapes, sizes, and forms. They can do jobs and tasks that may be too boring, repetitive, hard, or dangerous for humans to do. Robots use sensors and actuators to get to know their environment and respond based on the set of instructions (codes) that we give them!

Medical Robots Are Frontline Workers

The Rise of Disinfection Robots!

💡 Did you know?

Did you know that robots were a big help during the COVID-19 pandemic? From helping 3D print masks to cleaning hospitals and helping staff and sick patients, robots saved many human lives. "Violet," "Xenex," "XDBOT," and "UVD robot" are just some of these germ-zapping robots!

In spring of 2020, a study[1] by the Centers for Disease Control and Prevention (CDC) showed that millions of people in the United States had contracted COVID-19. Many robots helped keep our hospitals clean during this time. The disinfection robot called "Violet," designed by Akara Robotics, is one of them. You may be wondering what a disinfection robot is. When a sick person is in the hospital, tables, chairs, and other things in the room may become contaminated with germs. Cleaning these areas is important to keep germs from spreading and getting other people sick. Robots like Violet use special ultraviolet light to kill germs, or they spray disinfectants in rooms used by sick patients. This process is called disinfection. You may see one of these robots at your doctor's office soon!

Nurse Assistant Robots Are on the Frontline!

💡 Did you know?

Did you know that "Moxi," a friendly hospital robot created by Diligent Robotics, helped tired medical staff in their battle against COVID-19? Did you also know that in Japan, more than 5,000 nursing homes are using nurse assistant robots to help their residents? That is a lot of robots!

Robots can be nurse assistants, too. Cool, right? The "Moxi" robots[2-4] created by Dr. Andrea Thomas and Dr. Vivian Chu were used in many hospitals in Texas during the COVID-19 pandemic. Moxi is equipped with a robotic arm and a set of wheels on its base. Robots can be programed to help nurses with tasks and paperwork, run errands, and take some of the extra workload in busy hospitals! In Japan, engineers have created robotic nurses capable of providing care for senior citizens. Nurse assistant robots can take your temperature or blood pressure and even write down medical observations like how sick you are feeling or your body measurements. These robots then give their notes to your doctor! This way, the doctor is even more prepared to help you feel better.

Telepresence Robots Are Super Docs!

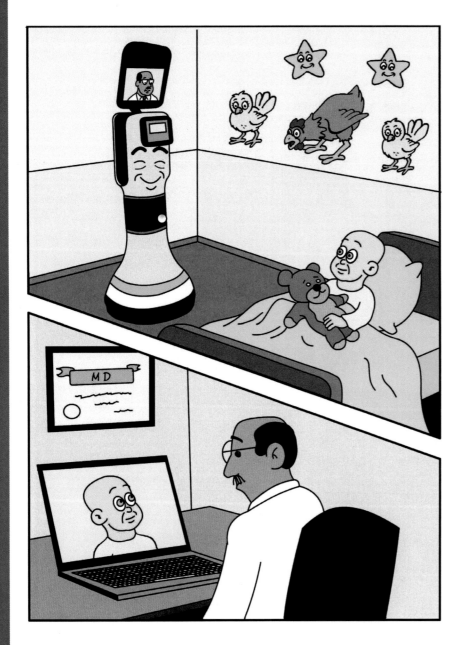

💡 Did you know?

Telepresence robots act as the eyes and ears of doctors and nurses in locations where medical specialists may not be available. Imagine living in a small town in India and talking to your doctor in the USA! In nursing care homes, telepresence robots can even entertain senior citizens!

You may have heard of surgical robots that help perform surgeries, but have you heard of telemedicine apps and telepresence robots? Telepresence robots[5] are computers on wheels that roll from room to room wearing cameras, lidar sensors (a type of sensor to map the environment), speakers, and microphones. They can be used in schools, in hospitals, in care homes, during natural disasters, and in business places, too. During the COVID-19 pandemic, with the help of telepresence robots, doctors were able to treat patients in another room or even a different city! These robots can help doctors talk to their patients, usually through a camera on the robot. The doctors can diagnose and perform check-ups on their patients without the risk of the doctors getting sick. Who knew robots could save doctors? For some grandparents isolated by COVID-19, telepresence robots can connect them with their loved ones and friends!

Rehabilitation Robots

Rehabilitation Robots Make a Better World!

💡 Did you know?

According to the World Health Organization[6], 2 billion people in the world live with some form of disability. Did you know that rehabilitation robots help make this world better for people with disabilities? You may have seen some kids or adults using robotic arms or legs to help them walk, run, or even play soccer.

A rehabilitation robot is a wearable machine that helps a person with disabilities. There are a few types of rehabilitation robots.[6-8] One type is an "assistive" robot that people use when their limbs don't work. Robotic exoskeletons (kind of like a shell) may use sensors and mechanical moving parts to improve the user's movement and independence. An example is a wheelchair-mounted robotic arm that a person can control using a chin switch. Another type of rehabilitation robot is called a "therapy" robot. Therapy robots such as "Paro" can reduce stress or help with physical therapy. In the past few years, a lot of progress has been made in helping autistic kids through robot interactions. These robots also allow therapists to study facial expressions or the way the body moves so they can improve the way they help their patients. Isn't that cool?

Service Robots
Are Everywhere!

Patrol Robots Are Cool Service Robots!

💡 Did you know?

Did you know that patrol robots are a kind of service robot? They were a big help during the COVID-19 pandemic. They use thermal cameras to measure people's temperatures from more than 16 feet away! During a pandemic, these robots may become our first line of defense against infectious diseases.

If you traveled with your family during COVID-19, you may have run into patrol robots at the airports. During a pandemic, it is extremely important to monitor crowded places like airports, malls, and restaurants, as we do not want more people getting sick or infecting others. Because of this, patrol robots have been employed to help frontline medical officers conduct disease prevention inspections. These robots can monitor if travelers are wearing masks or if they have a fever by using thermal imaging cameras and thermal detectors.[9-10] These robots will help make sure that the sickness does not spread more! Many businesses have installed robotic thermal cameras to screen workers for fevers. What would you do with a camera that could read people's temperatures from far away?

Retail Service Robots Are Helpful in Many Ways!

💡 Did you know?

Did you know that retail service robots like "Tally" help grocery store workers restock items, answer questions, and even do your shopping for you! Autonomous guided vehicles (AGVs) that move heavy loads around represent the largest group of retail service robots today! Amazon uses more than 100,000 robots in their warehouses to lift heavy loads and assist human workers.

It is not surprising that robots have started working in grocery stores and retail shops. You may see some of them in your neighborhood Walmart soon. Retail service robots[11-12] can perform many tasks to help store employees scan shelves, restock or check inventories, interact with customers, clean up spills, assist senior citizens with shopping, and even do the entire grocery shop for you! These robots have rotating lidar sensors to map their surroundings and high-resolution cameras like the Intel© RealSense™ depth cameras, so they can find their way around the store. They have many different types of sensors and cameras that help them detect obstacles and shoppers. Next time you are in the grocery store, watch for these amazing robots in action!

Delivery Service Robots Are Mini Self-Driving Cars!

💡 Did you know?

Did you know that companies like Starship Technologies and Kiwibot have already delivered more than 90,000 meals in the United States using delivery robots? They can also deliver groceries to your school or home. According to Door Dash, which uses delivery robots, there has not been even one instance of theft!

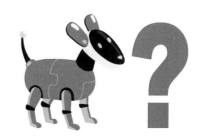

Imagine going to school and having your lunch delivered by robots during lunchtime! Food delivery robots[12-13] can quickly take an order for food via an app and deliver that food to your school, home, or work. Did you know that food delivery robots like "Pudu" use Intel© RealSense™ depth cameras and many sensors for mapping and driving around safely? They are like mini self-driving cars but are designed just to deliver food and supplies. Food delivery robots are also called cargo pods and can deliver food and supplies to the elderly and the disabled who cannot shop for themselves. Are you ready to see a delivery robot at your doorstep or at your school?

Consumer Robots Are in Our Living Rooms!

The "MarsCat" pet robot and "Roomba" robot vacuum cleaners[14] are everywhere! You may even have one at your house or maybe you saw one at your friend's house. These are examples of consumer robots. Anybody can buy one! Consumer robots can help clean the house, be cute pets, or serve as personal assistants. These robots can also work in retirement and care homes to help senior citizens stay connected and alert. "Walkamura" is a friendly helper robot that can act as a domestic assistant or an office receptionist. These little assistants help with day-to-day household tasks, from entertaining to organizing your schoolwork and family calendars. These robots are programmed with ultrasonic sensors, IR sensors, touch sensors, optical sensors, cameras, and AI technology to do many of the tasks that humans do. What would you train your helper robot to do?

Robots in Education

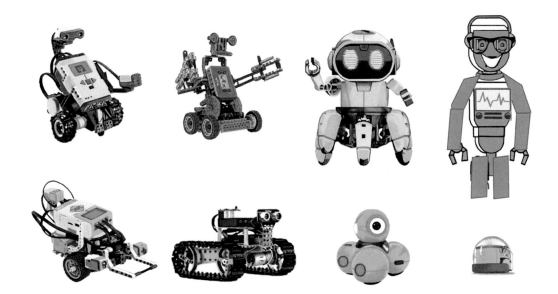

Teacher Robots Are Already Popular in Korea!

Did you know that in 2009, Japan developed the world's first robot teacher, "Saya"? Did you also know that in South Korea, the "Engkey" robot teaches English to elementary school students? Teacher robots enhance learning experiences for students and may use speech recognition technologies.

Can you imagine your teacher as a robot? Robots can be programed to learn a lot of information in just a few minutes and they can teach this information to students in a way that is easy for them to learn. The "Engkey" teacher robot[15] in South Korea uses voice recognition technology to help students practice English pronunciation, vocabulary, and dialogue. The "Pepper" robot and "iRobi" use facial recognition technology to ask kids about their mood and can make them laugh with silly jokes and movements. "Genibo" is a robot dog that teaches kids how to dance. The "iCAT" robot teaches kids to play chess, and the "Nao" robot helps kids improve their handwriting. The "Milo" robot teaches autistic kids! Teacher robots may use speech recognition technologies, advanced computer vision, and social signal processing technologies. They are very helpful in enhancing learning experiences, but of course they can't replace human teachers!

Education Robots Teach STEM Skills!

You may have used a VEX robot or LEGO EV3 robot at your school. These kinds of robots are a fun way to learn STEM (Science, Technology, Engineering, Math) and computer science.[16-18] STEM education is an absolute necessity to tackle our society's most pressing problems and robotics is a fun, hands-on way to learn to solve problems and build innovative and cool solutions! You will also find that programming or coding a robot at school is an exciting way to learn computer science and coding. Robotics is an inclusive field, which means that all kids can participate, including kids with disabilities and those who do not usually have opportunities to use technology. Maybe you and your classmates will invent the next amazing robot that can solve future problems!

Safety Inspector Robots

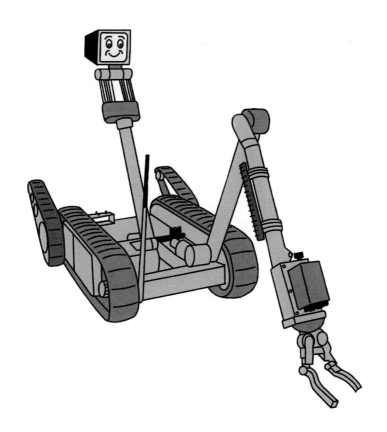

Robot Inspectors Perform Dangerous Jobs!

💡 Did you know?

Did you know that more than 4,000 "PackBots" are in military service today, helping with the inspection and detection of explosives, land mines, and bombs? These robots can safely access dangerous war zones to sense, analyze, and quickly disable devices that can hurt humans!

In war zones, robots can travel through rugged terrains and all-weather conditions to execute the very dangerous task of inspecting and removing land mines, toxic gases, radioactive materials, and explosives. They may be used for surveillance, sniper detection, neutralizing explosive devices, and providing medical support for injured solders. You may have seen police officers sending robots into a building where there might be a poisonous gas leak or a suspicious package. This way, the emergency workers and the people they are protecting can stay safe. The slithering "Snakebot" with a head-mounted camera,[20] developed by researchers at the Carnegie Mellon University, can inspect nuclear power plants, disaster zones, and archeological digs. When a job is too dangerous for humans, call in the inspector robots!

Explorer Robots

Aerospace Robots Explore the Universe!

💡 Did you know?

Did you know that the spacecrafts Voyager 1 and Voyager 2, launched by NASA in the summer of 1977 are famous robot explorers designed to conduct close up studies of Jupiter and Saturn? According to the NASA website, these unmanned spacecrafts and probes are over 15 billion miles away and still going! According to NASA and its partners SpaceX and Axiom Space Inc., we can soon expect to see humans and robots on space exploration tours!

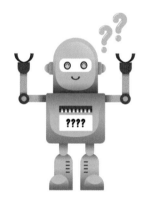

Can you believe that robots help us advance our knowledge about the universe? It is too difficult to send human astronauts into space for long periods of time, but robots can handle it. Their main job is to help astronauts and researchers by gathering information about our universe and conducting scientific experiments. They might collect soil samples on Mars or take pictures of our moon or other planets and galaxies. These robots carry sensors, cameras, and computers that are designed to survive hostile conditions. The "Robonaut 2" is a humanoid sent to the space station to help astronauts. "Perseverance," NASA's latest Mars rover, launched in February 2021, is carrying important scientific equipment, a small helicopter, robotic arms, and multiple drills and tubes to collect rock and soil samples to send back to earth so we can study evidence of ancient life on Mars![21-22]

Underwater Robots Explore the Ocean Floor!

💡 Did you know?

Did you know that the ocean explorer Robert Ballard used underwater robots to find the sunken ships, the Titanic and the Bismarck? Underwater robots can dive down more than 300 feet in water, unlike humans who can only dive 130 feet deep! The "Aquanaut" and the "Scarlet Knight" are some examples.

Underwater robots are referred to as sea gliders, or autonomous underwater vehicles (AUVs), or remotely operated vehicles (ROVs). They come in many shapes and forms[23-25] and they may look like submarines, snakes, or humanoid robots. Have you ever heard of Transformers? Then you are going to like the Aquanauts! These are submarine-like vehicles that travel around and take pictures under water, but then they can transform into humanoid robots to carry out more complex tasks or rescue operations. They can inspect the seabed, clean the ocean floors of trash, check oil pipelines, or operate valves and inspect oil leaks where it is too dangerous for humans to go. They are also used to create maps of the sea floor, find and record anything dangerous, and report any shipwrecks they might find!

Rescue & Recovery Robots

Rescue & Recovery Robots to the Rescue!

During a natural disaster or manmade disaster, rescue robots[26] can easily scale ladders, squeeze through holes, move rubble, survey damage, and look for survivors on air, land, or in water. They go where humans can't go! Whenever natural disasters like earthquakes, landslides, tsunamis, or flash floods hit, rescue robots are rushed to the scene alongside human first responders to help save people. In 2016, rescue robot "EMILY" helped save hundreds of people from drowning near the coast of Greece. NASA's "RoboSimian" can use its limbs and hands to complete many challenging tasks like turning a valve or picking up a drill. Rescue robot "Velox" can swim through water, skate along ice, and push through snow to save lives! Good thing robots are so tough!

Aerial Rescue & Recovery Drone Bots Are Cool!

💡 Did you know?

Did you know that drones were used in China to quickly deliver blood test samples to medical labs during the COVID-19 pandemic? They helped detect infection faster so patients could be treated sooner. Drones are proving to be extremely useful in places that humans cannot get to in a timely manner.

Drones have many abilities that help farmers, scientists, emergency workers, and even police officers do their jobs. They can scan large fields, take pictures to monitor crop damage, spray fertilizers, monitor irrigation systems for water leaks, deliver supplies for disaster relief, track storms, search for missing persons, track forest fires, survey archeology sites, and much more! They use lightweight sensors and cameras with data analytics software and AI technologies to gather information. After Hurricane Katrina, Professor Robin Murphy[27] and her team at Texas A&M University sent a swarm of mobile robots, called "unmanned aerial vehicles" (UAV), to survey the rubble and send pictures of the buildings and survivors to emergency responders. This was the first time UAV were used during a disaster! They are like superheroes!

Environmental Robots

Trash Recycling Robots Can Save the Planet!

Look who is helping keep the planet clean! These are trash collector, sorting and recycling robots that researchers are working on[28-29]. These robots can help collect, analyze, sort, and clean up trash! Using cameras, sensors, and AI, they can help separate recyclable and nonrecyclable waste. Recycling is a lot of work. By helping sort our trash, these robots will speed up the process and protect the planet! The trash and waste generated by humans has a negative impact on the environment on land and in the ocean. Engineers and scientists are looking for creative ways to solve this problem! It is a huge self-charging robot that can carry a lot of trash and never needs to be charged! For example, the "Row-bot" developed by the University of Bristol. It can swim, ingest microbes and pollutants in the water, and turn those into energy which then powers the boat's motor!

Robots in Agriculture

Agriculture Robots Can Help Plants Grow!

Agriculture is the field that focuses on farming and producing crops. Agriculture robots[30] can automate slow, repetitive tasks and make jobs like planning and planting crops, watering, and harvesting the food easier and faster. These robots use cameras with AI technology and vision software to check the health of the plant and sensors to check the soil conditions to help the plants grow. By having robots assist humans in agriculture, we can produce more food, faster. Since humans have more time to think and plan, the quality of food can improve, too! On factory farms, robots can be used for herding or milking cows. New technologies including drones, AI, and big data analytics are aligned to support farmers and the agriculture industry to provide food for everyone living on our planet!

Robots in Manufacturing

Industrial Assembly Robots Never Get Tired!

Industrial manufacturing robots[31-33] are hardworking robots that can do jobs that are repetitive or dangerous for humans to do. Robots can do some of the repetitive tasks such as painting, welding, assembling parts, and picking things up and placing them, and they can do dangerous jobs like cleaning windows on tall buildings. The great thing about robots with advanced sensors, AI technologies and fast processors is that they can do them safely, with better precision, and faster than human beings, and they never get tired or distracted. In many cases, robots like Amazon's warehouse robot "Kiva" work in a collaborative way with humans, with the robot being responsible for repetitive, menial tasks while the human worker completes the more complex tasks. These collaborative robots are also called "cobots."

Robots in Construction

Construction Robots Can Build with Precision!

💡 Did you know?

Did you know that the first ever 3D printed bridge is in the Netherlands? It was made by 3D printing robots. Robots can perform some of the same tasks as construction workers when building a new project. For example, robots can carry heavy loads and build walls for houses and buildings.

One of the most important things when constructing a building is that every measurement must be precise. Even little mistakes could mean the building won't be safe. It is important that everything fits into exactly the right spot. Construction robots[34] can make more precise measurements and cuts when building. The construction industry uses many different types of robots. You may have seen "SAM100," the construction robot, helping masons lay bricks for a wall. "Demolition" robots are safer and cheaper when it comes to razing old concrete buildings to make room for new buildings. In just half a day, an MIT – Massachusetts Institute of Technology – built robot can build an igloo shaped building, all by itself. As construction companies look to automate more and more tasks to improve efficiency and productivity, demand for construction robots will grow!

Humanoid Robots

Humanoid Robots are Here!

Did you know that humanoid robots[36-37] can have eyes, ears, and a nose, with a face that looks like yours or mine? Humanoid robots can act, talk, look, and function a lot like humans. They can be newscasters, soccer players, or even just have a friendly chat with you! Another cool thing about humanoid robots is that they're often used by scientists to study human behavior. Examples of humanoid robots include "Robonaut 2" the space explorer, "Pepper" the social robot, "Sophia" the duet-singing robot, "ASIMO" the world's most advanced humanoid robot, and "Kengoro" the exercising robot. The world's first Hindi-speaking and India's first realistic lip-syncing humanoid robot "Rashmi" can speak four languages: English, Hindi, Bhojpuri, and Marathi. Rashmi uses a linguistic interpretation system, AI, and visual data to interact with people.

Entertainment Robots

Entertainment Robots

💡 Did you know?

Do you know that Boston Dynamics has created robots that can perform stunts, flips, and somersaults, and land safely afterward? In many museums and amusement parks, entertainment robots can recognize faces, understand speech, and even entertain the museum's guests with stories about the history of the museum.

Having a boring day? You can now turn to an entertainment robot[37] to make you laugh or sing a song for you. These social robots are designed to interact with you and make you laugh or feel surprised. There are robots that have been programmed to do other entertaining things like dance, play soccer, or play a musical instrument. For example, the world famous humanoid robot "ASIMO," created by Honda, can perform a little dance to entertain people or have fun with you at a party! Some popular entertainment robots are Disney robots like "Na'vi Shaman," the humanoid robot "Sophia," and Toyota's "Partner" robots. You can even have little robot pets that entertain you at home!

Autonomous Robotic Vehicles

Self-Driving Robotic Cars Save Lives!

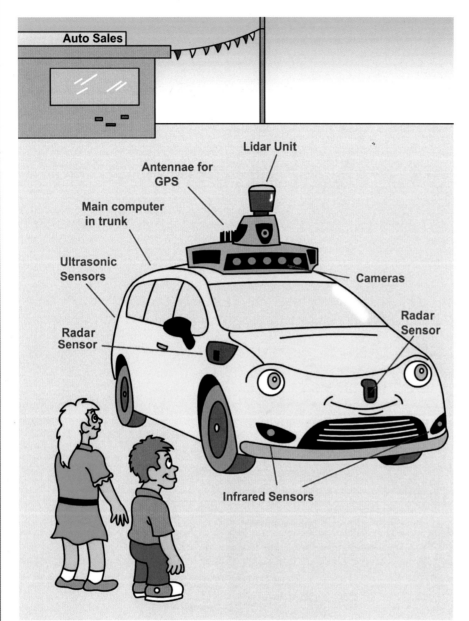

Auto Sales

Lidar Unit

Antennae for GPS

Main computer in trunk

Ultrasonic Sensors

Radar Sensor

Cameras

Radar Sensor

Infrared Sensors

Did you know?

Did you know that there are many cameras and sensors on self-driving cars offering 360-degrees of visibility? These cameras, sensors, AI, computer vision software, and superfast computers help the car drive safely. In 2015, a self-driving car from auto supplier Delphi drove from San Francisco to New York City, navigating 15 states and 3,400 miles all by itself!

It would be a lot harder to walk around safely if you couldn't see or hear! You have eyes and ears to help you get around. Self-driving cars have eyes and ears also. They are called sensors. Sensors are small machines that allow the car to look around and collect information. Self-driving cars can drive themselves and don't need human drivers. They are sometimes called "autonomous" or "driverless" robotic vehicles. Self-driving cars use several cameras and sensors, high speed computers, computer vision software and AI technology to see objects, people, animals, obstacles, traffic lights, signs, and the lines painted on the roads. All the information from the cameras, sensors, and GPS goes to a computer which creates a 3D map.[38] Using the map, the computer can decide which way to drive, when to brake or go faster, and how to steer. A self-driving car must gather a lot of information to get where it's going and keep its passengers (and other drivers) safe!

Will Robots
Take Our Jobs?

Will Robots, Automation, and AI Take Over All the Jobs?

💡 Did you know?

Did you know that some human jobs have been almost completely replaced by robots?

What will the future of jobs look like?

According to an Oxford University[39] study, more than 47% of all jobs could be automated by 2030. But don't worry, not all jobs can be performed by robots, automation, and AI!

You might be wondering if robots, automation, and AI will take over our jobs in future. They will! But this is not a bad thing. A long time ago, during a time called the Industrial Revolution, big, mechanical farm equipment replaced humans and horses on farms and made human lives better. People found new jobs, and now we are used to seeing tractors on farms instead of horses. Robots are good at jobs that are repetitive and predictable. By partnering with robots, humans can spend more time on complex jobs that humans are good at, such as designing, programming, fixing robots, testing, and innovating. During the COVID-19 pandemic, when human lives were in danger, robots saved many lives! The future requires problem solvers, collaborators, and innovators. Working side by side with the many friendly robots shown in this book would be a pretty cool job... don't you think?

References

1. Wortham, Jonathan, et al. "Morbidity and Mortality Weekly Report (MMWR)." CDC, 2020, www.cdc.gov/mmwr/volumes/69/wr/mm6928e1.htm?s_cid=mm6928e1_w. Accessed Jul. 16, 2020.

2. Diligent. "Moxi." Diligent Robots, 2020, diligentrobots.com/moxi. Accessed Jul. 16, 2020.

3. Bettencourt, Erica. "Robots Designed To Help Nurses, Not Replace Them." DiversityNursing Blog, 2017, http://blog.diversitynursing.com/blog/robots-designed-to-help-nurses-not-replace-them. Accessed Jul. 16, 2020.

4. Case Western Reserve University. "5 Medical Robots Making a Difference in Healthcare." Case Western Reserve University, 2019, online-engineering.case.edu/blog/medical-robots-making-a-difference. Accessed Jul. 16, 2020.

5. Ackerman, Evan. "Telepresence Robots Are Helping Take Pressure Off Hospital Staff." IEEE Spectrum, 2020, https://spectrum.ieee.org/automaton/robotics/medical-robots/telepresence-robots-are-helping-take-pressure-off-hospital-staff. Accessed Jul. 16, 2020.

6. World Health Organization. "World Report on Disability." WHO, 2011, www.who.int/disabilities/world_report/2011/report.pdf. Accessed Jul. 16, 2020.

7. Parobots. "Paro Therapeutic Robot." Paro, 2014, parorobots.com. Accessed Jul. 16, 2020.

8. Deshmukh, Smita. "Robotic Rehabilitation and Assistive Technologies to Revolutionize Physiotherapy." The Robot Report, 2019, www.therobotreport.com/robotic-rehabilitation-assistive-tech-revolutionize-physiotherapy/. Accessed Jul. 16, 2020.

9. Vergun, David. "Department Uses Thermal Imaging to Detect COVID-19." U.S. Department of Defense, 2020, www.defense.gov/Explore/News/Article/Article/2178320/department-uses-thermal-imaging-to-detect-covid-19/. Accessed Jul. 16, 2020.

10. U.S. Food and Drug Administration. "Thermal Imaging Systems (Infrared Thermographic Systems / Thermal Imaging Cameras)." FDA, 2020, www.fda.gov/medical-devices/general-hospital-devices-and-supplies/thermal-imaging-systems-infrared-thermographic-systems-thermal-imaging-cameras. Accessed Jul. 16, 2020.

11. Robotics Online Marketing Team. "Robots in Retail Stores are Making a Big Impact." Robotic Industries Association, 2017, www.robotics.org/blog-article.cfm/Robots-in-Retail-Stores-are-Making-a-Big-Impact/76. Accessed Jul. 16, 2020.

12. International Federation of Robotics. "Executive Summary World Robotics 2019 Service Robots." IFR, 2019, ifr.org/downloads/press2018/Executive_Summary_WR_Service_Robots_2019.pdf. Accessed Jul. 16, 2020.

13. Robotics Online Marketing Team. "Food Delivery Robots Take to the Streets." Robotic Industries Association, 2019, www.robotics.org/blog-article.cfm/Food-Delivery-Robots-Take-to-the-Streets/212. Accessed Jul. 16, 2020.

14. Ackerman, Evan and Erico Guizzo. "iRobot Brings Visual Mapping and Navigation to the Roomba 980." IEEE Spectrum, 2015, spectrum.ieee.org/automaton/robotics/home-robots/irobot-brings-visual-mapping-and-navigation-to-the-roomba-980. Accessed Jul. 16, 2020.

15. Ha-Won, Jung. "S. Korea Schools Get Robot English Teachers." Psys.org, 2010, phys.org/news/2010-12-skorea-schools-robot-english-teachers.html. Accessed Jul. 16, 2020.

16. VEX Robotics. "VEX Robotics." Vexrobotics.com, 2020, www.vexrobotics.com/. Accessed Jul. 16, 2020.

17. First Inspires. "First Lego League." First Inspires, 2020, www.firstinspires.org/robotics/fll/what-is-first-lego-league. Accessed Jul. 16, 2020.

18. Belpaeme, Tony, et al. "Social Robots For Education: A Review." Science Robotics, Aug. 15, 2018, DOI: 10.1126/scirobotics.aat5954. Accessed Jul. 16, 2020.

19. U.S. Bureau of Labor Statistics. "Employment in STEM Occupations." Bureau of Labor Statistics, 2020, www.bls.gov/emp/tables/stem-employment.htm. Accessed Jul. 16, 2020.

20. Ackerman, Evan. "What CMU's Snake Robot Team Learned While Searching for Mexican Earthquake Survivors." IEEE Spectrum, 2017, spectrum.ieee.org/automaton/robotics/industrial-robots/cmu-snake-robot-mexico-earthquake. Accessed Jul. 16, 2020.

21. Harper, Kelso, and Joel Goldberg. "How NASA's New Rover Will Search For Signs of Ancient Life on Mars." Science Magazine, 2020, www.sciencemag.org/news/2020/07/how-nasa-s-new-rover-will-search-signs-ancient-life-mars?utm_campaign=news_daily_2020-07-05&et_rid=17037140&et_cid=3389469. Accessed Jul. 16, 2020.

22. Clery, Daniel. "Three Dozen Alien Civilizations May Be Advanced Enough To Communicate With Us." Science Magazine, 2020, www.sciencemag.org/news/2020/06/three-dozen-alien-civilizations-may-be-advanced-enough-communicate-us?utm_campaign=news_daily_2020-07-05&et_rid=17037140&et_cid=3389469. Accessed Jul. 16, 2020.

23. Smithsonian Ocean Team. "Underwater Robots Explore the Ocean." Smithsonian Institution, 2010, ocean.si.edu/planet-ocean/tides-currents/underwater-robots-explore-ocean. Accessed Jul. 16, 2020.

24. Whyte, Jennifer. "Underwater Robots Are Helping to Save the Seas." Oceana, 2017. oceana.ca/en/blog/underwater-robots-are-helping-save-seas. Accessed Jul. 16, 2020.

25. Ackerman, Evan. "Meet Aquanaut, the Underwater Transformer." IEEE Spectrum, 2019, spectrum.ieee.org/robotics/humanoids/meet-aquanaut-the-underwater-transformer. Accessed Jul. 16, 2020.

26. Boyette, Chris and Tawanda Scott Sambou. "Robots, Drones and Heart-Detectors: How Disaster Technology Is Saving Lives." CNN.com, 2015, www.cnn.com/2015/08/24/us/robot-disaster-technology/index.html. Accessed Jul. 16, 2020.

27. Murphy, Robin. "These Robots Come To The Rescue After A Disaster." TED Women 2015. TED Talks, 2015, www.ted.com/talks/robin_murphy_these_robots_come_to_the_rescue_after_a_disaster. Accessed Jul. 16, 2020.

28. Johnson, Khari. "Alphabet's Trash-Sorting Robots Have Reduced Office Waste Contamination To 'Less Than 5%'." Venture Beat: The Machine, 2019, venturebeat.com/2019/11/21/alphabets-trash-sorting-robots-have-reduced-office-waste-contamination-to-less-than-5/. Accessed Jul. 16, 2020.

29. United States Environmental Protection Agency (EPA). "Advancing Sustainable Materials Management: 2015 Fact". Sheet https://www.epa.gov/sites/production/files/2018-07/documents/2015_smm_msw_factsheet_07242018_fnl_508_002.pdf. Accessed Jul.16, 2020.

30. Alexander, Donovan. "9 Robots That Are Invading The Agriculture Industry." Interesting Engineering, 2018, interestingengineering.com/9-robots-that-are-invading-the-agriculture-industry. Accessed Jul. 16, 2020.

31. Shaw, David and Intel Software. "Manufacturing Robots and AI." YouTube, uploaded by Intel Software, Mar. 21, 2019, www.youtube.com/watch?v=d1p3cJb8F7k. Accessed Jul. 16, 2020.

32. Robotic Industries Association. "What Are Collaborative Robots?" Robotics Online, 2020, www.robotics.org/collaborative-robots/what-are-collaborative-robots. Accessed Jul. 16, 2020.

33. Intel Newsroom. "2019 MWC: Intel's Smart Industrial Demo Shows a Safer Workplace." YouTube, uploaded by Intel Newsroom, Feb. 26, 2019, www.youtube.com/watch?v=AaNfMivB3dY. Accessed Jul. 16, 2020.

34. Matthews, Kayla. "5 Ways In Which Construction Robotics Is Disrupting the Industry." The Robot Report, 2019, www.therobotreport.com/construction-robotics-changing-industry/. Accessed Jul. 16, 2020.

35. The B1M. "The Construction Robots are Coming." YouTube, uploaded by The B1M, May 30, 2018, www.youtube.com/watch?v=nKGGHdl3NyQ. Accessed Jul. 16, 2020.

36. Silverstein, Steven and Katsu Yamane. "Humanoid Robots for Entertainment." Humanoid Robotics: A Reference, edited by Ambarish Goswami, and Prahlad Vadakkepat, Springer Nature, 2018, pp. 1-17, DOI: doi.org/10.1007/978-94-007-7194-9_111-1. Accessed Jul. 16, 2020.

37. Makimoto, Tsugio and T. T. Doi. "Chip Technologies for Entertainment Robots - Present and Future." Digest. International Electron Devices Meeting, Dec. 8-11, 2002, San Francisco, CA, DOI: 10.1109/IEDM.2002.1175768. Accessed Jul. 16, 2020.

38. SAE International. "Pittsburgh Meetups: Automated Vehicles." SAE.org, 2020, www.sae.org/automated-unmanned-vehicles/. Accessed Jul. 16, 2020.

39. Benedikt Carl, and Osborne Michael. "The Future of Employment" Published by the Oxford Martin Programme on Technology and Employment. https://www.oxfordmartin.ox.ac.uk/downloads/academic/future-of-employment.pdf Accessed Jul. 16, 2020.

Glossary

Robot: According to robots.ieee.org, a robot is an autonomous machine capable of sensing its environment, carrying out computations to make decisions, and performing actions in the real world.

AI: Artificial Intelligence (AI) is the ability of a machine to "think" and make decisions almost like a person would.

Computer vision: Computer vision is the system that is responsible for an autonomous vehicle's ability to "see" its environment. Examples are Artificial Intelligence (AI) software and microprocessors that can help process data from the sensors, and label and recognize objects and patterns.

Self-driving car: A self-driving vehicle can drive itself and doesn't need a human driver. There are many levels of driving automation. The Society of Automotive Engineers (www.sae.org) defines 6 levels of driving automation ranging from level 0 (fully manual) to level 5 (fully autonomous). Autonomous vehicles are typically classified at levels 3, 4, or 5 for driving automation.

Obstacle: An obstacle is something that blocks your way.

ADAS: An Advanced Driver Assistance System is a vehicle system designed to improve driving safety; it includes things like adaptive cruise control and lane departure warning.

Thermal Imaging: A device that uses heat signatures to form an image or video based on differences of temperature.

Consumer Robots: According to robots.ieee.org, Consumer robots are robots you can buy and use just for fun or to help you with tasks and chores.

Domestic Robots: According to robots.ieee.org, domestic robots are a type of service robots used for household chores.

Humanoid Robots: According to robotics.org, humanoid robots are professional service robots built to mimic human motion and interaction. An android is a humanoid robot designed to look similar in form to humans.

Data Analytics: Data analytics is the science of extracting meaning from raw data using specialized computer systems.

1. Can you name these robots?

_____   _____   _____

_____   _____   _____

2. Use the list of robot parts and label the robot. Make an educated guess based on what you have learnt!

Robot Brain, Camera, Sensors, Motors, Arms, Wheels

About the authors,
Anna Prakash-Ashton
& Elaina Ashton:

We are a mother-daughter team based in Chandler, Arizona, USA. We love technology and giving back to the community. We co-founded our non-profit organization, Education Empowers Inc., (www.educationempowers. org), to share our passion for STEM (Science, Technology, Engineering, Math), robotics, and sustainability education. As of Spring 2021, our curriculum and STEM-robotics clubs have reached children in more than 100 locations in Arizona.

Anna Prakash-Ashton is an engineer by profession and the winner of the prestigious Society of Women Engineers (SWE) "Prism" award in 2017 for her contributions to technology and STEM advocacy for girls, young women, the underrepresented, and underserved children. Anna has several technical publications and patents covering sensors, displays, optoelectronics, and semiconductor packaging materials and processes.

Elaina Ashton is currently enrolled at Arizona State University, Barrett Honors college, majoring in the engineering field. She is the winner of the Cox Connect2STEM award, Junior Achievement of Arizona's 18 Under 18 award, and the SWEnext - Local Innovator award for STEM outreach.

We sincerely hope that this material and our other books in this series can help you to start a STEM-robotics club or a maker club in your local community or school. Well... what are you waiting for?

Would you like to read more about self-driving cars, sensors, robotics, drones, AI, and other exciting STEM fields? Check out our other books coming soon at https://just-empower.com

Made in the USA
Las Vegas, NV
26 April 2021